Chipper

CHIHUAHUAS

SASSY! ALERT! ENERGETIC!

TINY! BRIGHT! LOVING!

ABDO
Publishing Company

Katherine Hengel

Consulting Editor, Diane Craig, M.A./Reading Specialist

Published by ABDO Publishing Company
8000 West 78th Street, Edina, Minnesota 55439.

Printed in the United States of America,
North Mankato, Minnesota
052010
092010

 PRINTED ON RECYCLED PAPER

Editor: Liz Salzmann
Content Developer: Nancy Tuminelly
Cover and Interior Design and Production:
  Anders Hanson, Mighty Media
Illustrations: Bob Doucet
Photo Credits: Shutterstock

Library of Congress Cataloging-in-Publication Data
Hengel, Katherine.
 Chipper chihuahuas / by Katherine Hengel ; illustrated by
Bob Doucet.
    p. cm. -- (Dog daze)
  ISBN 978-1-61613-377-1
 1. Chihuahua (Dog breed)--Juvenile literature. I. Doucet,
Bob, ill. II. Title.
  SF429.C45H46 2010
  636.76--dc22
                        2010001576

CONTENTS

The Chihuahua	3
Facial Features	4
Body Basics	5
Coat & Color	6
Health & Care	8
Exercise & Training	10
Attitude & Intelligence	12
Litters & Puppies	14
Buying a Chihuahua	16
History of the Breed	18
Tails of Lore	20
Find the Chihuahua	22
The Chihuahua Quiz	23
Glossary	24

The CHIHUAHUA

Chihuahuas are very small dogs from Mexico. They may be tiny, but they have a lot to offer! Chihuahuas have a lot of energy. They are also very **affectionate** and love their owners.

FACIAL FEATURES

Head

Chihuahuas have small, round heads. The shape is called an "apple dome."

Teeth and Mouth

They have short, pointed **muzzles**. Their small teeth close in a scissors bite.

Eyes

A Chihuahua's eyes are full, round, and set far apart.

Ears

Chihuahuas have large ears that stand up on their heads.

4

BODY BASICS

Size

Chihuahuas weigh less than 6 pounds (3 kg). They are 6 to 9 inches (15 to 23 cm) tall.

Build

Chihuahuas are lean and sturdy.

Tail

Chihuahuas have long tails. They often curl over their backs.

Legs and Feet

Chihuahuas have thin legs and **dainty** feet. Their toes don't spread out much.

COAT & COLOR

Chihuahua Fur

Chihuahuas can have smooth or long coats. The smooth coats are soft and glossy. The fur is short and close to the dog's skin. It thins out on the head and ears. Their tails and necks may be a little furrier.

Long coats are less common. Chihuahuas with long coats have soft, long fur. It can be wavy or straight. The fur on their ears, tails, feet, and legs is longer than the rest of their coat.

CREAM FUR

FAWN COAT WITH WHITE MARKINGS

CREAM COAT

BLACK COAT WITH WHITE MARKINGS

Chihuahuas come in many different colors and coats. The photos on these pages show just a few examples.

FAWN FUR

BLACK FUR

RED FUR

WHITE COAT WITH FAWN SPOTS

BLACK, WHITE, AND FAWN COAT

RED AND WHITE COAT WITH BLACK SABLING

HEALTH & CARE

Life Span

Most Chihuahuas live about 12 to 18 years.

Grooming

Smooth coats do not need much grooming. Long coats should be brushed several times a week. Chihuahuas should be bathed once a month. However, it's important to keep water out of their ears.

VET'S CHECKLIST

- Have your Chihuahua spayed or neutered. This will prevent unwanted puppies.

- Visit a vet for regular checkups.

- Ask your vet about which foods are right for your Chihuahua.

- Clean your Chihuahua's teeth and ears once a week.

- Make sure your Chihuahua gets enough exercise.

- Trim your Chihuahua's nails about once a month.

EXERCISE & TRAINING

Activity Level

Chihuahuas are lively little dogs! They have a lot of energy, and they love attention. They don't need a lot of space to exercise. They are happy in the city or small apartments. They do just fine in hot weather.

Obedience

Chihuahuas are great companions. They are extremely **loyal** and **sensitive**. It takes patience to train them, but they respond well to gentle training.

A Few Things You'll Need

A **leash** lets your Chihuahua know that you are the boss. With a leash, you can guide your dog where you want it to go. Most cities require that dogs be on leashes when they are outside.

A **collar** is a strap that goes around your Chihuahua's neck. You can attach a leash to the collar to take your dog on walks. You should also attach an **identification tag** with your home address. If your dog ever gets lost, people will know where it lives.

Toys keep your dog healthy and happy. Dogs like to chase and chew on them.

A **dog bed** will help your pet feel safe and comfortable at night.

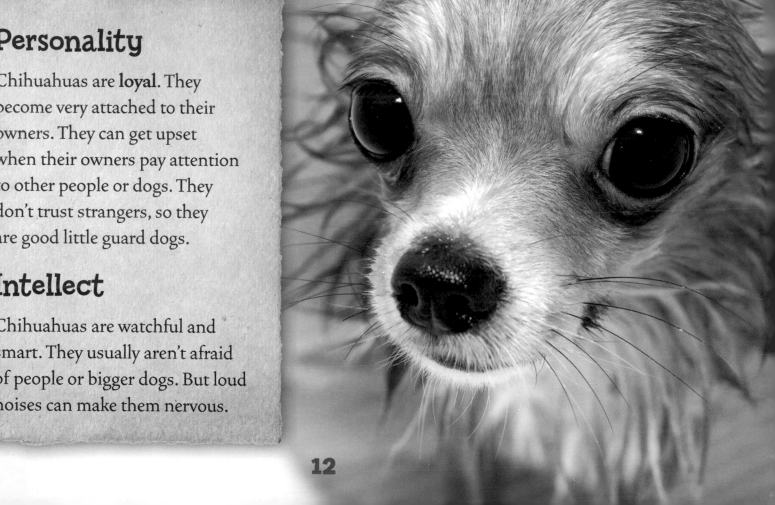

ATTITUDE & INTELLIGENCE

Personality

Chihuahuas are **loyal**. They become very attached to their owners. They can get upset when their owners pay attention to other people or dogs. They don't trust strangers, so they are good little guard dogs.

Intellect

Chihuahuas are watchful and smart. They usually aren't afraid of people or bigger dogs. But loud noises can make them nervous.

All About Me

Hi! My name is Chuck. I'm a Chihuahua. I just wanted to let you know a few things about me. I made some lists below of things I like and dislike. Check them out!

Things I Like

- Playing inside
- Protecting my owner
- Getting a lot of attention
- Curling up under a blanket to sleep
- Going wherever my owner goes

Things I Dislike

- Seeing my owner with other animals
- Being alone a lot
- Being outside in cold weather

LITTERS & PUPPIES

Litter Size

Female Chihuahuas usually give birth to two to three puppies.

Diet

Newborn pups drink their mother's milk. Chihuahuas can begin to eat soft puppy food when they are about five weeks old.

Growth

Chihuahuas should stay with their mothers until they are about nine weeks old. They reach their adult size when they are about a year old.

BUYING A CHIHUAHUA

Choosing a Breeder

It's best to buy a puppy from a **breeder**, not a
pet store. When you visit a dog breeder, ask
to see the mother and father of the puppies.
Make sure the parents are healthy,
friendly, and well behaved.

Picking a Puppy

Choose a puppy that isn't too
aggressive or too shy. If you crouch
down, some of the puppies may
want to play with you. One of them
might be the right one for you!

Is It the Right Dog for You?

Buying a dog is a big decision. You'll want to make sure your new pet suits your lifestyle.

Get out a piece of paper. Draw a line down the middle.

Read the statements listed here. Each time you agree with a statement from the left column, make a mark on the left side of your paper. When you agree with a statement from the right column, make a mark on the right side of your paper.

I want a dog that can handle hot weather.	☐	☐	It is often cold outside where I live.
I want a dog that barks at strangers.	☐	☐	I don't want a dog that is suspicious of strangers.
I don't mind bathing and brushing my dog.	☐	☐	I don't want to have to groom my dog a lot.
I live alone and don't have children or other pets.	☐	☐	I have a big family, and we have other pets.
I want a dog that is very attached to me.	☐	☐	I don't want a needy dog.
I want a dog that can come along when I go out.	☐	☐	I don't need to bring my dog everywhere with me.

If you marked more X's on the left side than on the right side, a Chihuahua may be the right dog for you! If you have more X's on the right side of your paper, you might want to consider another breed.

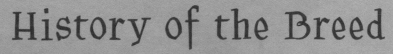

THE LITTLE DOG FROM MEXICO

The Chihuahua is a very old **breed**! Chihuahuas have been popular for hundreds of years. They came from Chihuahua, Mexico. That's how they got their name!

Chihuahuas were **sacred** to many Mexican Indians. European explorers that came to Mexico in the 1500s also liked Chihuahuas. Christopher Columbus even wrote about them in a letter to the King of Spain! Today Chihuahuas are popular all around the world.

SMALL BUT SACRED

A Techichi was a small dog that looked like a Chihuahua. They are probably related! The people who lived in Mexico hundreds of years ago thought these small dogs were **sacred**.

They believed Techichis could help their spirits after they died. **Archaeologists** have found carvings of small dogs in tombs and pyramids in Mexico. The dogs look just like Chihuahuas!

FIND THE CHIHUAHUA

A

B

C

D

THE CHIHUAHUA QUIZ

1. Chihuahuas come from Mexico. **True or false?**

2. Most Chihuahuas live only 8 years. **True or false?**

3. Chihuahuas need a lot of space to exercise. **True or false?**

4. Chihuahuas are good guard dogs. **True or false?**

5. Chihuahuas like being outside in cold weather. **True or false?**

6. Chihuahuas usually give birth to 2 to 3 puppies. **True or false?**

Answers: 1) true 2) false 3) false 4) true 5) false 6) true

GLOSSARY

affectionate - being loving and tender.

aggressive - likely to attack or confront.

archaeologist - one who studies the remains of people and activities from ancient times.

breed - 1. to raise animals that have certain traits. A *breeder* is someone whose job is to breed certain animals. 2. a group of animals with common ancestors.

dainty - small and delicate.

loyal - faithful or devoted to someone or something.

muzzle - an animal's nose and jaws.

sacred - very important and deserving of respect, especially as part of a religion.

sensitive - aware of how others are feeling.

About SUPER SANDCASTLE™

Bigger Books for Emerging Readers
Grades K–4

Created for library, classroom, and at-home use, Super SandCastle™ books support and engage young readers as they develop and build literacy skills and will increase their general knowledge about the world around them. Super SandCastle™ books are part of SandCastle,™ the leading preK–3 imprint for emerging and beginning readers. Super SandCastle™ features a larger trim size for more reading fun.

Let Us Know

Super SandCastle™ would like to hear your stories about reading this book. What was your favorite page? Was there something hard that you needed help with? Share the ups and downs of learning to read. We want to hear from you! Send us an e-mail.

sandcastle@abdopublishing.com

Contact us for a complete list of SandCastle,™ Super SandCastle,™ and other nonfiction and fiction titles from ABDO Publishing Company.

www.abdopublishing.com • 8000 West 78th Street
Edina, MN 55439 • 800-800-1312 • 952-831-1632 fax